THE BLUE AND BUFF

THE BLUE AND BUFF

PORTRAIT OF AN ENGLISH HUNT

John Minoprio

SWAN·HILL PRESS

Photographs and text by John Minoprio.

The illustration on page 9 is reproduced by permission of
the Duke of Beaufort and the Trustees of the late Lionel
Edwards. The extracts from Lionel Edwards' books are
reproduced by permission of the Trustees.

First published in the UK in 1992
by Swan Hill Press
An imprint of Airlife Publishing Ltd.

British Library Cataloguing in Publication Data
  A catalogue record of this book is available
  from the British Library.

ISBN 1 85310 264 4

Printed by Kyodo Printing Company (S'pore) Pte Ltd.

Swan Hill Press
An imprint of Airlife Publishing Ltd.
101 Longden Road, Shrewsbury SY3 9EB

This book is dedicated to
Ian Farquhar
and to those who carried the
Beaufort horn before him.

I feel very honoured that John Minoprio has asked me to write the foreword to this book.

The first part records the influence of the 8th and 9th Dukes of Beaufort, both giants in the annals of foxhunting, but I am sure all will agree even they do not compare with my predecessor - Master - whose total dedication and skill will be remembered for ever.

John Minoprio also describes all the many other characters past and present, who have done so much to ensure that our hunt still thrives.

I, sadly, have recently given up hunting, which I miss more than I can say, having been lucky enough to have had 41 years of total enjoyment, but as long as my eyes last, I will be able to indulge my nostalgia looking at these wonderful photographs.

Beaufort

Badminton   August 1991

PREFACE

In *My Hunting Sketch Book* Lionel Edwards includes a picture of the Duke of Beaufort's near Hawkesbury Monument and writes:

'The number of sketches, good, bad and indifferent which I have perpetrated of this pack must be considerable'.

It was Lionel Edwards' books which gave me the idea that I might attempt a book of photographs of The Duke of Beaufort's Hunt. I hope Lionel Edwards, known as the 'master artist of the horse in colour and line' would approve. He certainly understood the photographer's difficulties. In his introduction to Frank Meads' superb book *They Meet at Eleven* 'L.E.' writes:

'Artist's licence enables the painter to ignore unpleasant features and extraneous details, and to record only the absolute essential details; but the camera has an unpleasant way of recording everything, and a telegraph pole or advertisement on a wall will mar what is in all other respects a good picture.'

How true. Reviewing photographs for this book, I was especially pleased with one showing hounds arriving for a meet at Badminton House, until I noticed a single green wellington boot apparently protruding from the underside of the Master's horse.

This is a picture book, not a definitive portrait. I have merely tried to photograph those things which caught my eye, and to show the beauty of the Beaufort Hunt country, its light and shade, and that hunting and its supporting activities, bring pleasure to many. Apart from the pictures in stable and kennel, the photographs record events as they happened and were not set up.

My sincere thanks must go to everyone who has helped me - especially His Grace The Duke of Beaufort and his Joint Master, Captain Ian Farquhar, the late Major Gerald Gundry, Antony Brassey, John Mackenzie-Grieve, Major and Mrs Ronnie Dallas, Brian Gupwell, Brian Higham, Charles Wheeler, Peter and Liz Noest, Major Tim Morley, Lady Dill, Anne Hewson, Sir Michael Farquhar, Richard Meade, Michael Clayton, Jane Gundry, Julie Hoskins, Mrs Pope, Zia Kruger, Grant Barnes, Sue Godwin, Jack Windell, Mrs MacInnes, Mrs Marsh, Colin Stainer, Tim Smith, Sally Sutton, Auriol Culverwell, Didi Saunders, Jim Gilmore, Peter Sidebottom, Jane Holderness-Roddam, Lucinda Green, Virginia Leng, Alison Murray-Wells, Clare Tomlinson and Bernard Weatherill Limited.

I am deeply grateful to Gilbert and Pam Walshaw who, with great generosity, endless patience, constant good humour, and seemingly inexhaustible hospitality, have conveyed me in chauffeur driven comfort the length and breadth of the country in search of photographs. I cannot thank them enough.

Lastly, I must thank Alastair Simpson and John Beaton of Swan Hill Press - not only for all their advice and help with the production, but for their decision to publish the book in the first place. It is they who have made this book possible.

JOHN MINOPRIO
Threapwood
1992

Vincent Brooks,Day & Son, Lith.

THE DUKE OF SPORT - It is appropriate, in view of the 8th Duke of Beaufort's all round sporting interests, that I should chance upon this cartoon in the catalogue of a specialist seller of cricket books.

THE DUKES OF SPORT

CAR FOLLOWER SUPREME - THE 9th Duke of Beaufort.

'It is a capital country and such a lot of room. The Vale is delightful, too. Hounds race over it in fine style. We get large fields some days . . . '

So wrote Will Dale to his former Master Mr. F.J.S. Foljambe soon after coming to Badminton as Huntsman to the 8th Duke of Beaufort in 1896. The 8th Duke had widespread sporting interests — hunting, racing, carriage driving, cricket, he was President of the MCC and editor of the Badminton Library. The modern game of Badminton was invented in his house, and the caricature of him by Spy which appeared in *Vanity Fair* was rightly inscribed 'the Duke of Sport'.

Nearly one hundred years on, it is still a capital country and hounds race over it in fine style, with large fields on some days, too.

And this, surely, is a great achievement. For the Twentieth Century, with its turmoil and change, has been hard on foxhunting. Yet, it flourishes, and nowhere more splendidly than at Badminton, where the 5th Duke of Beaufort began hunting the fox in preference to deer in 1762.

Today there are between thirty and forty horses in the Badminton stables, eighty couple of hounds in kennel, two hundred subscribers to the Hunt, twelve hundred members of the Beaufort Hunt Club, and two hundred and seventy members of the Beaufort Hunt Pony Club. A Saturday mounted field can total one hundred and fifty, while the number of registered cars is eighteen hundred. The Duke of Sport would no doubt approve.

His son certainly would, for the sketch by Lionel Edwards shows the Hunt's most famous car follower and it is of the 9th Duke of Beaufort in his Ford. Forced to give up hunting after an accident in 1919, he had first started hunting his father's bitch pack two months before his 21st birthday in 1868. It was said of him in his car that 'given a horn, and a few couple of hounds, he could still catch a fox as well as any huntsman in England'.

All reports confirm that he had an extraordinary gift for knowing which way a fox had gone, and whenever hounds checked, there he was, sitting silently in his car accompanied by his chauffeur, and his dog, smartly turned out in a coat of Blue and Buff.

MASTER - Henry Hugh Arthur FitzRoy Somerset 10th Duke of Beaufort, K.G., P.C., G.C.V.O., photographed during the 1963-4 season. 'I have devoted a large part of my life to foxhunting.'

The sketch was done after the Duke's death, and his widow had it reproduced as a memento for the Duke's many tenants and friends. Lionel Edwards wrote 'It is no artist's invention, for many a time I saw him as depicted'.[1] That the artist had succeeded was confirmed by the Duchess of Beaufort herself for she was quoted in *Horse and Hound* as considering it 'the best portrait of my husband in existence'. While in the book *Shires and Provinces*[2] it was simply described as 'a speaking likeness of the Duke and his son'.

And that was appropriate, for in his memoirs[3] the 10th Duke would write:

1 Famous Foxhunters, Eyre & Spottiswoode (1932)
2 Published by Eyre & Spottiswoode 1926
3 Country Life Books 1981

'Lionel Edwards often came to stay at Badminton. He was very much my father's protege. My father gave him great encouragement when he was a young man for he needed not only persuasion but a certain amount of backing before deciding to dedicate himself to a life as a writer and artist.'

These Victorian noblemen, the 8th and 9th Dukes of Beaufort, were certainly remarkable for the widespread affection in which they were held. It was said of them that they were incapable of a mean or ungenerous action. Reading about them, the same words recur — courtly, charming, genial, a natural attraction for young and old, kindness. Their generous nature appealed to all classes and they were held in as high esteem by their fellow Dukes as by their estate workers.

And if the Duke could have named his own successor to the Badminton inheritance, he could not have done better than his rightful heir, the late 10th Duke of Beaufort, who would write 'I have devoted a large part of my life to foxhunting'.

But that could as well be said of his father and his grandfather, for these three Dukes shared a passion for hunting which is surely unique in one family. It by no means follows that sons enjoy their father's favourite sports, especially when you reflect that the second son of the 8th Duke was a songwriter. The spirit of these Dukes, an aura of good sport and generosity, persists at Badminton today.

My first photograph in this book is of the late Duke of Beaufort and that is as it should be. Foxhunting was his inheritance and his destiny. He was given a pack of harriers on his eleventh birthday and was called 'Master' from that moment on. Like his father, he began hunting the family pack as Marquess of Worcester at the age of 21, and continued for forty-seven seasons.

He was a worthy successor to The Duke of Sport because, like his grandfather he was President of the MCC, and he continued the family tradition of inviting famous players to take part in matches at Badminton, including Wally Hammond, described by John Arlott as 'among the half dozen finest cricketers of all history'.

My picture below was taken during the 1963-4 season and it shows the Duke moving off after a meet at Fosse Lodge. He is happily setting out on one of the 3895 days recorded in his diary when he carried the horn. His hounds cluster round his horse and his Blue and Buff field ride behind him. Clearly, he is enjoying himself - his enthusiasm as strong as ever after over 40 years hunting hounds.

But perhaps like his father and grandfather before him, he always seemed to be enjoying the occasion. I remember him at Horse Shows, judging hunters at Richmond, congratulating The Household Cavalry's Best Turned Out Trooper at Windsor, or

THE PREMIER FOXHUNTER IN ENGLAND - The 10th Duke of Beaufort, moving off from a meet in the 1960s. His great friend Sir Peter Farquhar, Master of the Portman 1947–1959, is among many well-known Beaufort members present.

going round the stands, talking to exhibitors at The Horse of the Year Show, or greeting his guests at the pre Badminton Horse Trials Cocktail Party. He put everyone at ease. No wonder Lady Apsley inscribed her book *Bridleways through History:*[1]

'To Henry, 10th Duke of Beaufort, K.G. in token of good sport Past, Present and Future'.

Then the sport was foxhunting, but the event riders of today would find this an equally fitting dedication, for they owe much to the Duke's generous and far-sighted decision to establish the Three-Day Event at Badminton in 1949. His Beaufort sporting ancestors would surely be amazed that this twentieth century Duke - he was born in 1900 - would make Badminton familiar to horsemen and women all over the world. And that this Blue Riband of the Three Day Event, would draw a vast crowd of two hundred thousand, one of the biggest in any spectator sport.

Apart from having devoted much of his life to foxhunting he held many official and Royal Appointments. He was Master of the Horse for forty years, responsible for the Queen's safety on all State and formal occasions whenever Her Majesty was mounted or in a carriage, with the right, as senior to all on parade, to ride at her side. A close friend of the Royal Family, his wife was the niece of Queen Mary, who stayed at Badminton throughout the Second World War.

This association with the Royal Family prompted the Duke, helped by the Crown Equerry, Lt. Col. Sir John Miller, to persuade Prince Charles and Princess Anne to start hunting. The Prince of Wales' sustained enthusiasm for the sport is a comfort to all who hunt today, when foxhunting finds itself under attack.

The Duke died at the age of eighty-three, the oldest of all the Dukes of Beaufort, in 1984 and was succeeded by his cousin.

The 11th Duke of Beaufort, as David Somerset, competed first at Badminton on the Olympic horse Countryman which he had bought in 1958. According to one report he slipped a place in the showjumping, but still finished 'a commendable seventh'. The following year Beaufort supporters sensed a very special victory was in the air when Countryman, defying the appalling ground conditions after torrential rain, completed a brilliant cross country round to make up fifteen places and take the lead for the final day. The margin was small, but the man who had worn the Blue and Buff for the dressage on the first day stood higher than many big names, including Sheila Wilcox, Ted Marsh, Derek Allhusen and the Olympic Gold Medallist himself, Frank Weldon.

But a famous home win was not to be. Countryman had one fence down to give Sheila Wilcox a record three consecutive Badminton triumphs. Even so, those who strive for the Mitsubishi Motors Trophy today should spare a thought for their host, who, when the going got tough, got going, and came so near.

1 Hutchinson and Co. 1936

The Duke joined the Mastership of his family pack in 1974 and has hunted whenever he could, although his profession as director of a world famous art gallery has meant that he has not been able to hunt as much as he would have wished.

A gifted horseman, he used his cross country riding skills to great effect in the hunting field. Those who tried to follow him as Beaufort Field Master could readily understand why he beat the hot favourites round the Badminton course.

My picture shows him, an immaculate figure, at a meet at Fosse Lodge in 1989. It was said that 'an Englishman looks his best in hunting kit'. Although the Duke is admired for his elegant dress sense, I think the photograph could persuade that this was true.

The Duke has assumed an immense responsibility for the great house and the estate. One often views the house from a distance - and its grand proportions look fine - draw near and its scale is daunting. But with its park, its deer, its magnificent stable yard and its kennels, all roads in the Duke of Beaufort's country seem to lead to Badminton House. And the Duke, together with the Duchess, have been absorbed in a programme of extensive and impressive development, both to the house and to the estate as a whole The Duke is deeply interested in planting and conservation and is most generous in allowing access to the Park so others may see and enjoy it.

Upholding the traditions of his family as patrons of sport, the Duke has generously provided the British Three Day Event Team with splendid accommodation for both horse and rider at Badminton so that they can train under the most ideal conditions.

With the Three Day Event bigger than ever, with the hunting flourishing, and the Estate enjoying renewal, the 11th Duke's contribution is already formidable. Inflation and taxation did not trouble the mind of the 9th Duke when, as Marquess of Worcester, he was enjoying the 16 mile point known as the Greatwood Run in 1871. Things are rather different today, and it is wonderful to see what is going on at Badminton, under the guiding hand of one who is descended from John of Gaunt.

In this century the Hunt and the Beaufort family have had many friends but none truer than Gerald Gundry who joined as Secretary in 1938. For over forty years, first as Secretary, then as Joint Master, from 1951 to 1984, he continued in the role of Chief of Staff and Ambassador at Large. Apart from the war, when he served with great distinction, winning the DSO in the Italian campaign, 'the Major' dedicated his life to the Hunt, its country, and its supporters. He hunted the mixed pack two days a week during his Mastership and when he gave up riding he took to his Land-Rover, going to all the meets, and invariably seeing the action from the best possible vantage points.

Immensely tall and thin, he had the huge hands of a countryman who had also rowed for Eton. But he wrote letters in a free flowing hand, and I especially remember his kindness when I had the idea for this book. He was immediately encouraging, and I was able to enjoy his help, his hospitality and his wonderful sense of humour. And to talk with him about Lionel Edwards, for there on his wall was the artist's famous picture of 'The Dauntsey Vale' - the original, a gift from the late Duke who wrote of the debt he owed Gerald Gundry, describing him as 'more than my right arm'.

Needless to say, Tetbury Church was surely never so full than on 11 January 1991 for the thanksgiving service for the life of Major Gerald Gundry. The Duke of Beaufort, in his address on that occasion, captured the spirit of the Major's single minded dedication to the Hunt perfectly. Hunting was his life.

Another key figure in the post war era is Major Ronnie Dallas who retired as Secretary in 1987 after thirty years in the post. A 3rd Hussar, and an international showjumper who competed with British teams in Rome, Lisbon and Madrid, Major Dallas pays tribute to his wife Sylvia, the daughter of Colonel Guy Cubitt, the founder of the Pony Club. 'A Hunt Secretary needs a keen wife to do the work', he admitted. That their partnership was successful was proved by the huge crowd which gathered when hounds met at Badminton House for the presentation to mark Major Dallas's retirement.

Major Dallas recalls that any reputation that the Hunt had for being stand-offish, and exclusively for the rich, was false. He can remember blacksmiths and chimney sweeps coming out hunting while there was tremendous support from the hunting farmers on the Badminton Estate. And he is grateful for the kindness and generosity shown him by the two Dukes of Beaufort whom he served as Secretary. Today, he is Chairman of the Hunt Club which raises money for the Hunt and other charities. And he hunts regularly, adding that Captain Farquhar is showing very good sport and the hunt horses still look superb.

Brian Gupwell retired as Kennel Huntsman in 1989. A Huntsman's son, Brian is a very fine horseman who hunted the hounds for eighteen seasons in his twenty-two year career with The Duke of Beaufort's. He came from the Eridge and had what many would concede to be a daunting and unenviable task for, when he arrived at Badminton in 1967, he had to take over from the man who had carried the horn for forty-seven years and whose car bore the number plate MFH 1.

Brian Gupwell's long innings shows he won the full confidence of the late Duke and Major Gundry. Seeing him in later years, he seemed a perfect model for a Huntsman to a Duke. Tall and slim, immaculately turned out, he had the natural elegance of professional sportsmen in the days before flannel gave way to man-made fibre and 'leisure' became an industry. His 15 Peterborough Champions for the Beaufort Kennel set the seal on a lifetime of hunt service. In spite of having endured hip operations he still enjoys hunting today.

The emphasis on hunting in the Beaufort family is certainly remarkable, and it created the need for good horses which persists today. No visitor to Badminton can fail to marvel at the grandeur of the main stable yard, with its forty-five boxes.

In the old days the Beaufort hunted six days a week, sometimes seven. What an undertaking. And the 9th Duke was a very big man requiring very big horses. These filled the 'twenty boxes' stable at Badminton for the Duke always had three horses out each day and liked to have seventeen or eighteen horses for his own use plus a couple of strong cobs. These horses fascinated Lionel Edwards. In 1932 he writes:

'Their breeding must have been, even more than with most hunters, a matter of chance. In size they were carthorses; in quality they showed more "blood" than I have ever seen in horses at all approaching their size. They reflected, I think, remarkable judgment on the part of both buyer and seller. Seeing as I do an immense number of hunters every year, I believe it would be impossible to find horses like those today, - it must have been a matter of great difficulty even then'.

Four days hunting a week requires some horse power and the search for good horses never stops, but the famous Dr Tom Connors of Upper Broughton, Leicestershire, supplies many of them - fine Irish horses that really look the part.

And today, four days a week is still impressive and my photographs endeavour to show something of the Beaufort scene and those who enjoy it. I hope that, in years to come, this book may revive memories of the good fun had following today's Duke of Sport in everything but name, Captain Ian Farquhar.

AT WORCESTER LODGE - The 10th Duke of Beaufort, having exchanged his green coat for the Blue and Buff when he gave up hunting hounds, rides at the head of the field on a fine February day in 1976. The huntsman is Brian Gupwell and the whipper-in is Denis Brown.

CROSS-COUNTRY SPECIALIST - The 11th Duke of Beaufort at a meet at Fosse Lodge in 1989. As David Somerset, one show jump down cost him the Badminton championship after a cross-country round that eclipsed Olympic stars. His style and boldness out hunting were widely admired by the Beaufort field.

'THE MAJOR' - Gerald Gundry receives a presentation set of glasses to mark his retirement as Chairman of The Point-to-Point Committee in 1989. Colonel Sir Hugh Brassey, former Chairman of the Hunt, is holding the microphone. A much-loved figure in the Beaufort country, Major Gundry worked singlemindedly and selflessly in the cause of the Hunt for over fifty years.

LONG SERVICE HONOURED - A Meet at Badminton House is reserved for special occasions. One was the retirement of Major Ronnie Dallas after thirty years as Secretary in 1987. A huge crowd gathered to honour Major Dallas and thank him for all that he had done. The Duke of Beaufort presented him with a silver figure of a fox which he received modestly. Then someone in the crowd shouted 'Hold it up!' and the photograph records the moment. The picture shows, from left to right, Mr. Antony Brassey, Chairman of the Hunt, Mrs. Dallas, who was presented with a bracelet, Captain Ian Farquhar MFH, Major Dallas, The Duke of Beaufort, Major Gerald Gundry, the Duchess of Beaufort and Mrs. Farquhar.

THE PROFESSIONAL - A professional for over forty years, Brian Gupwell, Huntsman 1967–1984, Kennel Huntsman 1985–1989, had the unenviable task of taking over after The Duke of Beaufort's legendary forty-seven years hunting hounds.

BUSMAN'S HOLIDAY - Brian Gupwell enjoys himself jumping one of the fences for fun after the Royal Wessex Yeomanry Ride. A superb horseman, Brian retired in 1989 but still goes hunting today even after enduring hip joint operations.

GENTLEMEN AND PLAYERS - Taking over the microphone to pay tribute to Brian Gupwell on his retirement in 1989, Major Gerald Gundry, a renowned raconteur and after dinner speaker, makes amusing reference to Brian having to work with an amateur huntsman. The joke's on Captain Farquhar and he takes it well. The Duke of Beaufort, who has just presented Brian with a cheque and a silver hunting horn, relishes yet another sample of 'The Major's' wit.

HUNTING DYNASTY - Born into the aristocracy of foxhunting, Captain Ian Farquhar LVO MFH cannot remember the time when he did not go hunting. The son of Lt. Col. Sir Peter Farquhar Bt DSO MFH, famous hound breeder and friend of the 10th Duke, he was appointed Master and Huntsman to The Duke of Beaufort's in 1984 after thirteen highly successful seasons with the Bicester.

Seeing him jump off a road, with deceptive ease, you remember what he has to do hunting hounds four days a week from November to March. To 'show sport' puts him in the entertainment business and he well understands the need to bring in the box office. But he wins all hearts with his dashing drive and enthusiasm and gives those that try to keep up a tremendous run for their money.

Captain Farquhar's wife, Pammy Jane, is herself the daughter of a Master of Foxhounds. A bold and brilliant rider in the first flight of the Beaufort field, she is seen here with her sister Sally, who wears the primrose collar of the Wynnstay Hunt, and Ronnie Dallas at a meet at the home of her brother-in-law, Sir Michael Farquhar Bt.

Determined to stay out to the end of the day, Captain Farquhar's daughter Victoria, rides alongside her father after he has blown for home. As befits a member of the Farquhar family, Victoria and her sisters Emma and Rose have inherited their parents' love of hunting.

THE SECRETARY - 'I draw the line at a phone on my saddle' said John Mackenzie-Grieve, 'but my tape recorder is more reliable than my memory.' Beset by messages and requests on all matters of Hunt administration and finance, the Secretary wisely carries this modern aide-memoir. But he fears it goes counter to the tradition of foxhunting upheld in this photograph by his gleaming top hat and highly polished boots. The message giver is Gilbert Walshaw, a devoted car follower and friend of the Hunt, at a meet at Sherston.

'Every time we set foot off the road we are somebody's guest' said John Mackenzie-Grieve. As Secretary in the field his main task is to see that stock don't get out and to get any fences repaired properly. A former Secretary to the Pytchley, John Mackenzie-Grieve succeeded Major Ronnie Dallas in 1987. 'He is most conscientious' said his predecessor.

FIELD MONEY - *'Field money, which originally started with Irish packs of hounds is a very excellent institution . . . and is used to help pay damage or other claims. Most Hunts can easily collect from £5 to £10 a day in this way, making a very useful addition to the hunt funds at the end of the season.'* So wrote Cecil Aldin in 1933. The principle applies just as well today, although inflation raises the figures quoted by 8000 per cent. Here, a young follower reaches to place her field money in the Secretary's outstretched hand.

THE HUNTSMAN'S EYES AND EARS - 'I should be wherever the Captain isn't, be his eyes and ears . . .' said Charles Wheeler. His job in the field is to help his huntsman, to watch, to listen and to inform. The Hunt Servants carry whistles, while the Huntsman's voice and the language of the horn report progress to his whippers-in.

KENNEL HUNTSMAN - Born into a farming family Charles Wheeler has completed eight seasons with the Duke of Beaufort's having come from the Bicester with Captain Farquhar. He served his apprenticeship with the North Cotswold starting as kennel man and terrier man. Appointed Kennel Huntsman on Brian Gupwell's retirement in 1989, he has eighty couple of hounds under his supervision. He is seen walking out near Badminton.

CALLING FOR HOUNDS - Giles Wheeler, the second whipper-in, concentrates on his prime task of calling hounds on when they spread out while drawing or fall behind. He is watching and mentally counting them all the time, and when hounds may cover up to one hundred miles in the course of a day he must, for if a hound goes missing it's his job to find it.

STUD GROOM - Coming from a Yorkshire family of coachmen and gamekeepers, Brian Higham has had thirty three seasons at Badminton, having started as Second Horseman and Second Man in 1959. He was promoted Stud Groom in 1966 and is responsible for the largest private hunting yard in the country which is virtually unchanged since 1880. Brian, who insists on 'good old-fashioned stable routine', describes Badminton, away from the busy roads, with its grand house, park and stables, as being in a 'kind of cocoon'. But he adds 'It's a wonderful place and the Duke is a wonderful man to work for. He likes to see things done properly - he gives you a free hand, backs you up to the hilt, and yet is always ready to advise if you have a problem. I am very proud to work for him just as I was very proud to work for the late Duke. Captain Farquhar keeps his horses here, too, which is a pleasure. The horses go very well for him and of course I remember his father and mother, Sir Peter and Lady Farquhar, who used to come and hunt here often'.

Brian gets a tremendous thrill out of hunting and when time allows, and providing all's well in the yard, he likes to go out for half a day. 'The hounds are going very well and I think hunting is in a very healthy state - you have only to look at all the car followers to see the entertainment they get.' But, sounding a word of warning, 'People must be more realistic on costs . . . there are not enough good horses and it takes a long time to make a young horse. There aren't the nagsmen about these days - and young farmers haven't the time. It's the horses that are so expensive, but it's no use looking back'.

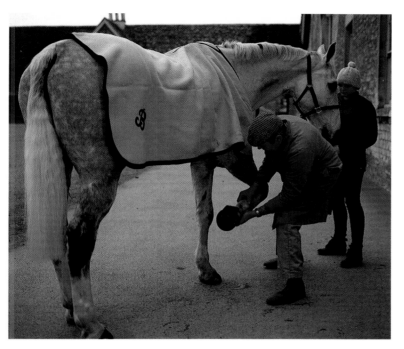

THE DAY AFTER - Post hunting routine is strict. Here, Brian Higham checks hunters for soundness. With each horse hunting two half days a week, Brian has to keep a constant watch over them. And he avoids enormous vet's bills by dealing with the everyday things himself. The Badminton stables are high, an average of 15 feet with plenty of room for air to circulate. Warm in winter and cool in summer, the horses live in what must surely be the equestrian version of a five star hotel.

'GOOD OLD-FASHIONED METHODS' - Brian Higham using the singeing lamp to deal with cat hairs in the Spring. It looks a tricky business, but note the horse's calm expression. The groom is Jan Wilkinson. 'All horses like it' said Brian, 'and it makes a lovely job, you can always tell . . .'.

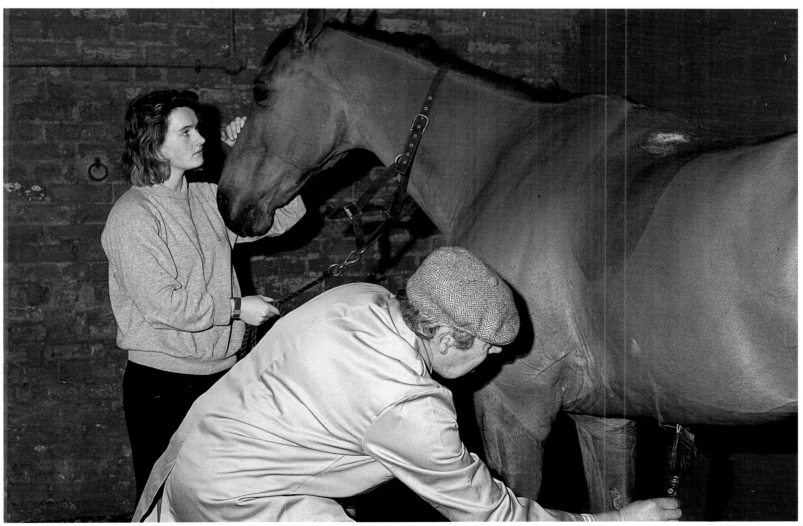

A CHAMPION'S CASE FOR HUNTING - 'Hunting is a great introduction for jumping and it provides a lovely base for making them sure-footed' says eventing champion, Ginny Leng, who lives and hunts in the Beaufort country. And her record speaks for itself. She has won the Badminton Championship twice and Burghley a record five times. She was World Champion in 1986 and European Champion in 1985, 1987 and 1989, as well as being a team Silver and individual Bronze Medallist at both the Los Angeles and Seoul Olympic Games.

Ginny explains: 'Hunting has a vital part to play, not only in eventing, but in racing too, and it provides the clue to a lot of British success in riding horses over fences. Our overseas competitors do not have this advantage. Hunting teaches a horse to look after itself, to cope with any type of going, and to acquire the much needed mental attitude to keep going forward.

And it's a wonderful way to teach children to ride cross-country. There's no question about it - they become street-wise and develop natural flair and security in the saddle.'

Ginny enjoys hunting her eventers if their personality is right for the hunting field. It's no fun, as with any horse, if they get too wound up. And she goes hunting to help horses who may have lost confidence, or have done a lot of competitive work. Sometimes, they need the bit of light entertainment which hunting gives them.

Her World Championship entry Griffin has hunted this season with both the Duke of Beaufort's and the Pytchley as part of a 'refreshment' course. And when her champions retire, as in the case of Priceless and Night Cap, they go hunting and love it.

Ginny says that the National team training facilities at Badminton, so kindly provided by the Duke of Beaufort, are marvellous. She admits 'we're spoiled to death in the glorious stables. And the Duke takes such a tremendous interest, it's great'.

SIX TIMES WINNER - No reference to the Badminton Horse Trials would be complete without recalling the remarkable record of Lucinda Green MBE, six times Badminton winner on six different horses. Here she is, in her familiar colours, during the Steeplechase phase, riding Mrs Murdoch's Willy B in 1988.

Lucinda enjoyed hunting with the Beaufort from time to time when she wanted to give her event horses some fun. On one occasion she was cantering down to a tiger trap on Be Fair, the chestnut who gave her her first Badminton win in 1973. The eager Beaufort field jostled Be Fair as he neared the fence and the illustrious event horse hated this. His response was to stop dead.

Among the rough and tumble of riders who cannoned into his back was an immaculately veiled lady riding side-saddle, who roundly ticked off the 19 year old future World Champion. Greatly embarrassed, Lucinda realised that Be Fair had offended none other than the Duchess of Beaufort herself!

PARADE OF HOUNDS - The scene as the Duke of Beaufort's hounds parade on the final day of the Badminton Championships in 1991. Captain Farquhar doubles his horn as he takes hounds to Giles Wheeler's holloa at the far end of the ring. Charles Wheeler is on the bay in the foreground.

PRESENTATION - Scarlet coats are rare in Beaufort Country, but they abound as the Badminton prize winners line up to receive their rosettes. The Princess of Wales and Prince William are accompanied by the Duke of Beaufort, Sam Whitbread, Chairman of Whitbread's sponsors of the Event for thirty years, Hugh Thomas, Director, and Jane Gundry, Secretary of Badminton Horse Trials. Rodney Powell heads the line on The Irishman II and has every reason to look happy after his first Badminton triumph.

ROYAL PATRONAGE - The Duke of Beaufort brings the Royal Princes into the ring to see his hounds and the photographers move in. The Duke thanks his Joint Master and Kennel Huntsman for the parade which marks the link between fox hunting and eventing at Badminton.

AT GRASS - On an early morning in July, two chestnuts graze contentedly in a classic Cotswold setting in front of Easton Grey House.

THE MARE AND FOAL - Horses are bred on many farms in the Beaufort country. Here mares and foals enjoy the midsummer grass at Cape Farm overlooking the Park at Badminton. It is the home of the Smith family, keen and successful breeders of hunter chasers.

THE BROOD BITCH - Barrier '89 with her whelps, five bitches and two dogs, four weeks old, sired by Ranger '90. Barrier is by Berkeley Freshman '84, an outcross which has proved highly successful in the Beaufort kennel. Barrier is an outstanding bitch in her work. On her first morning's cub-hunting she left cover behind a strong cub and managed to hunt and kill it singlehandedly. But here she is a picture of patient gentleness as she cares for her brood, possible future stars who may inherit her talent.

THE VIXEN - 'In all our heritage of mammals there is no other that occupies such an important place in the life of the countryside' wrote the naturalist, Frances Pitt. 'The wildcat, pine marten, and the polecat have long been refugees in the wild hills, while the fox remains with us, and that not as a rarity, but as an honoured guest in nearly every wood'.[1] This vixen, still feeding her cubs, roams untroubled by hounds during foxhunting's close season. She can breed in peace, protected as an honoured guest - but the click of a shutter set at 1/500 second startles her, and in an instant she is gone.

[1] Chapter 'Animal Life' from Nature in Britain (B.T. Batsford 1936)

EMINENT JUDGES AT THE PUPPY SHOW - *Two of the most famous Masters in the post-war era Captain Ronnie Wallace and Captain Charles Barclay have judged at The Duke of Beaufort's Puppy Show for over twenty years The Puppy Show is a social occasion and a thrill for those tireless puppy walkers who see their mischievous charges win prizes.*

But the wettest June in memory takes its toll and for once summer dresses and panama hats give way to raincoats and golfing umbrellas for this mid-summer event. Here the doghounds have arrived for final selection and the judges must sort them out. Charles Wheeler throws the biscuit and the alert young hounds give chase. Giles Wheeler is on the right. Note the bowler hats among the spectators. They are worn by hunt servants from neighbouring packs who are the guests of the Joint Masters on this occasion.

PETERBOROUGH - The Duke of Beaufort's has won countless prizes at the Peterborough Royal Foxhound Show and, from the rosettes on Charles Wheeler's arm, this year is no exception. But the year is nevertheless a special one for the Duke of Beaufort is President, an office held five times by previous Dukes of Beaufort since 1878.

The picture shows the final judging of doghounds in the Fitzwilliam Hound enclosure at the East of England Show in July. The Duke of Beaufort's has already been successful with Daystar in the class for unentered hounds but on this occasion the Wheatland takes the Championship. The President, accompanied by the Duchess of Beaufort, watches the judging. His Joint Master, Captain Ian Farquhar, is on his right.

CUBHUNTING: SUNRISE - Cubhunting starts as soon as the corn is cut. It begins at first light to take advantage of the better scenting prospects that the cold conditions of early morning allow. But this September scene looks as though it might be the prelude to a hot day.

CUBHUNTING: STEAMING HORSES - Perhaps not ideal cubhunting conditions, but what a morning for a ride.

DUCAL GRANDEUR - The main yard at Badminton. Forty-five boxes, each 12' x 12', with the yard itself the size of half a football pitch.   Built in the 19th Century there was accommodation for a total of one hundred and twenty horses before carriages gave way to the motor car.   Even today, there are over thirty horses in the stables during the season and the figure rises to eighty plus during the four days of the Badminton Horse Trials. The 'twenty box yard', filled by the 9th Duke's hunters, is on the right of the picture.

EXERCISE - Drive a car near Badminton in the hunting season and the lanes seem full of riders. But roadwork is a regular part of the hunter's regime, and is of great benefit at conditioning time when they come up from grass in July. Then they have six weeks roadwork to get them 'legged up'. Hunters may do as many as forty days in a season and must be produced hard and fit.

TAIL PIECE PERFECTION - The old saying 'a head like a lady and a bottom like a cook' still applies. But traditional skill and attention to detail shows in this perfectly pulled tail. And the photograph emphasises the well muscled up hind quarters that a hunter needs, and only good stable management can maintain.

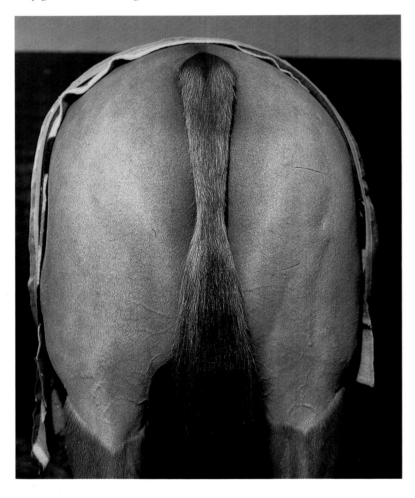

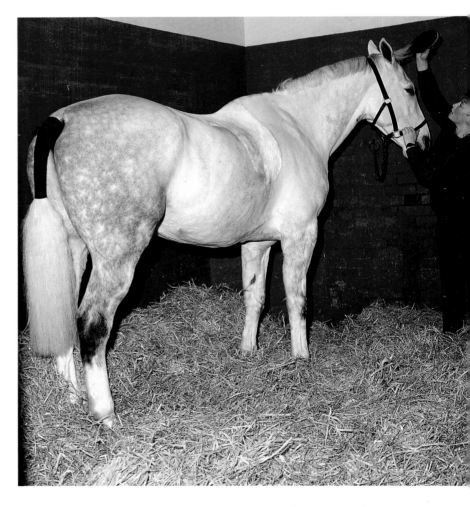

HER MASTER'S HORSE - A girl groom 'does' the Master's horse at Badminton. There are ten girls in the yard. Brian Higham, who has trained countless young people in horsemanship, describes them as 'conscientious and enthusiastic'. Note the bedding of deep straw.

VITAL TASK IN SAFE HANDS - Gleaming saddles proclaim Dick Williamson's pride in his work. He served the Dukes of Beaufort for over fifty-six years - forty-one as Woodsman and fifteen as the Tackman. His domain is a magnificent panelled tack room, its temperature controlled between sixty and seventy degrees F, to allow the tack to dry slowly.

There are about sixty saddles, old and new, in the tack room. All are immaculately cared for. The importance of this behind scenes support cannot be over stressed. A day's hunting is very hard on saddles and bridles - defective tack is downright dangerous. Here, Dick uses glycerine saddle soap, but if the tack is wet he will apply Neatsfoot oil after the first cleaning.

THE FARRIER - Bernard Tidmarsh visits the Badminton yard twice a week. 'If you haven't got a good farrier you get nothing but problems and Bernie's one of the best - a real master' said Brian Higham. The photograph shows him shoeing a hunter hot in the classic way. When he puts the hot shoe on the foot the burnt places show him where he must rasp to ensure a perfect fit.

THE SADDLER - When Henry Ford launched his Model T 'Town Car' in 1915 the prospects for saddlers on both sides of the Atlantic didn't look too good. But seventy-five years on the Malmesbury saddler is well placed in the Beaufort country. Here, Philip Barnes is seen repairing one of the Hunt saddles. Hunting saddlery must be stronger, the bridles wider. All saddlery at Badminton is inspected regularly - and a policy of preventive maintenance keeps Mr Barnes busy, and the age old craft survives.

HUNTING MORNING - THE BADMINTON YARD - Grooms ride around the yard under Brian Higham's watchful eye before handing over their charges to the Masters and their guests. The Kennel Huntsman and Second Whipper-in stand by ready to mount.

'A HUNTING WE WILL GO' - Surrounded by exuberant hounds, Captain Farquhar leaves the Kennels on a hunting morning. Note the fox weather-vane. The 9th Duke had the weather-vanes turned round, specially weighted so that the fox points down wind, the way be usually runs.

THE BLUE AND BUFF - The distinctive blue livery of the Dukes of Beaufort harks back to the Lancastrian colours of azure and gold. The founder of the family was the fourth son of Edward III, Duke of Lancaster - Shakespeare's 'Old John of Gaunt, time-honour'd Lancaster'. The right to wear 'The Blue and Buff' is in the personal gift of the Duke of Beaufort.

ELEGANT BYSTANDERS - And the horses look good too. A pair of bays, their gleaming coats the product of fitness and good grooming, stand with well-mannered calm at a meet at Long Newnton.

THE YOUNGEST FOLLOWER - There's nothing like starting young. Certainly the Dukes of Beaufort believed in this. When the biographer T.F. Dale talked to the children at Badminton House, he was told 'we are not allowed to hunt more than four times a week until we reach the age of five'.

THE OLDEST FOLLOWER - 'I'd throw a brick in the air and if it came down, I'd go hunting' said Jack Windell who had his first day with the Duke of Beaufort's on a grey cob which delivered milk to Hullavington Station in 1924. He's been hunting ever since.

A long-time and much respected farmer, Jack believes in tradition and the need to maintain it. He was privileged to go on to the corner of a cover to see the fox away for the 10th Duke. This privilege was not granted to many. Jack recalls the Duke's irritation with the over zealous hollowing of others, 'all right, all right, keep your mouth shut, that isn't the only fox in England!'

Jack's hunting diaries record the many days he has had. 1960 found him hunting on 31st March while in 1976 he had fifty-nine days. 'I had some of the best hunting in the world, behind the best man in the world, in the best time of my life - and no one can take that away from me . . . '

The picture shows three generations of the Windell family - Jack, his son Michael, and granddaughter Anne. Jack wears a wellington boot after breaking his leg in a hunting accident - but nothing would deter him from going out, as always, on 'the day before the point-to-point'.

THE OPENING DAY - There is a definite thrill about the first day of the hunting season proper. New faces, new horses, what will the new season bring? Here on a sunny November morning, with poppies to mark Armistice Day, the field moves off from Worcester Lodge. The day was a good one . . . including a five and a half mile point, about ten miles as hounds ran.

SATURDAY - Hounds moving off from a meet at Fosse Lodge. The huge gatherings of old no longer prevail and one hundred and fifty mounted followers on a Saturday is now looked on as a big field. Rather different from the days when the 8th Duke would entertain a thousand people to breakfast and four to five hundred to lunch. In 1860 2,200 people were mounted at a lawn meet. Nevertheless the enthusiasm of today's two hundred subscribers remains as strong as ever.

TAKING HOLD - Eager to gallop as the first field beckons, this chestnut bounds forward, his pent up power like a coiled spring. The strength, energy and stamina of a fit hunter are not always appreciated - and that they go well for women is another phenomenon, even if three times as many girls ride than boys.

54

BOTTLENECK - *The field forced into the bottleneck of a gateway when hounds are not running. Followers emerge in single file to ride the headland. Saturday near Luckington.*

SATURDAY FIELD MASTER - *The Hunt owes a debt to all its Field Masters and none more so than to Peter Sidebottom, whose role as Saturday Field Master is daunting. He has to keep the farmers happy - they don't want to see damage - he must help the Huntsman - he wants room to do his job - and he must look after the interests of a pressing hundred and fifty strong field, many of whom hunt only one day a week and want some fun. And of course, day in and day out, he must lead from the front.*

It's a difficult juggling act. 'You have to concentrate all the time, and for six hours you can't let up for a moment' says Peter, a London merchant banker and point-to-point rider who moved to the Beaufort Country from Kent twenty years ago. 'And if you lose your temper you're done for. You have to try and make sure that they enjoy their sport'

He admits 'Ian Farquhar is very good across country - a difficult man to follow.' But then I have a feeling that Peter Sidebottom is very good across country, too.

. . . The Field he must lead.

58

HRH THE PRINCE OF WALES - His Royal Highness The Prince of Wales photographed on the darkest of days at Westonbirt. Hounds have just hit the line and Prince Charles is in what the golf commentators call 'position A'. Although the Prince now lives in the Beaufort Country it was from a meet at The Kennels, Badminton that he had his first day's hunting in 1975. He was following Royal custom for not only had his great uncle, the Duke of Windsor, hunted with the Beaufort as Prince of Wales, but in 1867 the then Prince of Wales, later King Edward VII, came to stay at Badminton to hunt.[1] The Prince wears a distinctive royal hunting coat based on the Windsor Uniform introduced by George III. He adopted this as standard when he began to hunt regularly with many different packs.

1 The Badminton Tradition by Barry Campbell
  Michael Joseph 1978

JAM AT WIDLEYS - Car followers are such great supporters of hunting that one feels one should be 'to their faults a little blind, and to their virtues ever kind'. But this Saturday jam at Widleys, near Sherston, shows that the 'motorised battalion' can cause problems. A register of cars is kept on a computerised database and the current total is 1800.

GILBERT AND PAM - *Forced to give up work to look after his invalid mother, Bath ice cream maker and restaurateur, Gilbert Walshaw noticed in the local paper that hounds were meeting at the Blathwayt Arms, Lansdown. Out of curiosity, and for something to do, he decided to wrap his mother up warmly in the car and go - he's been hooked on hunting ever since.*

Shown here near Sopworth, Gilbert, and his wife Pam, like 'to go where the other cars aren't'. He says 'we see more foxes that way' and his loud holloa 'Gone over!' is one Captain Farquhar can trust. Gilbert and Pam's hospitality is legendary, their generosity is only matched by their love of hunting. Has a simple notice of a meet in The Bath Wilts Chronicle and Herald *ever gained the Hunt two more loyal supporters? I doubt it.*

Jake, finding things a little slow, asks 'When can we go to the car wash?' But mother, Fiona, a Monday follower, remains totally absorbed.

61

KEEN SPECTATOR - Taking over the driver's seat to get a better view, an inquisitive fox terrier shows the intelligent interest that his breed would imply.

THE PROFESSIONALS - *Seasoned campaigners, hunt terriers bear the scars of battle. One ignores the camera, the other meets the lens with a fixed stare and growling disapproval. The late Duke of Beaufort in his book* Foxhunting *wrote 'no one can really tell a game terrier just by looking at him, though a prominent dark eye is a good pointer'.*

THE ROYAL WESSEX YEOMANRY CROSS COUNTRY RIDE,
THE FIRST FENCE -The Duke of Beaufort is Colonel of The Royal
Wessex Yeomanry and the annual ride is held at Cape Farm,
Badminton. Here the forty-two starters in 1990 approach the first fence
in something of a cavalry charge.

THE WINNER -
   'One was a Lancer, long of limb
   And it took a good 'un to ride with him.
Major Christopher Marriott, of the 17th/21st Lancers, riding Crunch,
comes home as overall winner for the second successive year. The
sixteen fence course was planned by Lt. Col. Frank Weldon.

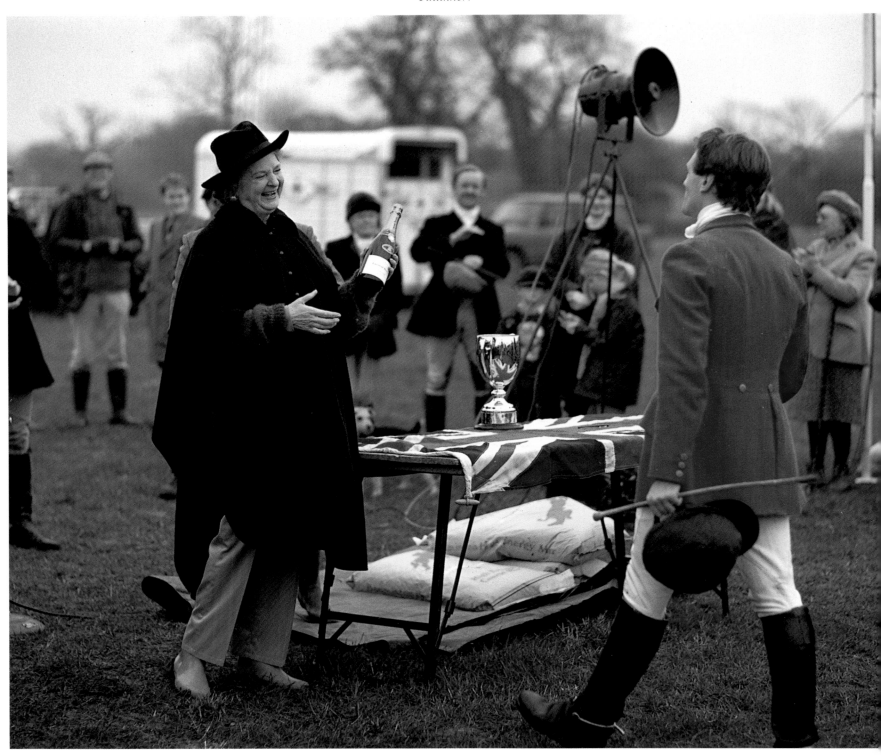

FORMER WINNER - Miss Joanna Lowsley-Williams from Chavenage after winning the race in the Beaufort Hunt colours in 1988.

THE HUNT BALL - The Hunt Ball takes place at Grittelton House in early December and is very much a part of the Hunt calendar. With around six hundred tickets sold this is no small affair, and the Committee works tirelessly to ensure that it is a success. The picture shows dancing in progress, although I'm not sure what has happened to the Hunt Chairman's spectacles!

NO HOUR OF LIFE IS LOST - Recalling his love of riding while at Sandhurst, Winston Churchill wrote: 'No hour of life is lost that is spent in the saddle'. Those who hunt the morning after the Ball will surely agree . . .

BOXING DAY - A large crowd gathers each year for the Beaufort Boxing Day meet at Worcester Lodge, the beautiful building designed by William Kent and built in 1735 at the north end of the park three miles from Badminton House.

HAPPY OCCASION - On Boxing Day the spectators outnumber the riders by ten to one, and this means that up to two thousand people can greet the Joint Masters and hounds on this happy occasion, a tradition for many not to be missed.

FROST - A meet at the Kennels on a cold January morning. Captain Farquhar is discussing the chances with Mr Derek Sidebottom while terrier man Fred Ind is in the background. Note the Welsh hound on the left, then in her 10th season hunting.

FOG - Meeting at 10.45 in Sherston, the Hunt adjourns to a fogbound field, there to wait until 2 o'clock before deciding to abandon the day. Here hounds and riders walk round like prisoners at exercise.

RAIN - A cold torrential morning does not deter the enthusiastic Saturday field. They just turn up their collars . . . and keep smiling as Caroline Appelbe proves.

A BREAK IN THE WEATHER - THE RAINBOW - And how lucky that Michael and Sue Pike, who farm at Sherston, were in the right place for the picture.

GOING TO THE MEET AT EASTON GREY - A bright gleam of morning sunshine makes the picture possible as two hunt members ride on to a meet at Easton Grey. The Cotswold stone buildings are typical of many found in the villages of Beaufort country and give the area an enduring appeal.

LAWN MEET - A traditional scene at Easton Grey House, the Georgian mansion of Mrs Didi Saunders, who is the host for this meet. There has been a house on this site since 1236 and Easton Grey was mentioned in the Doomsday Book. It has an early link with hunting for in the reign of Edward II, John de Grey held the Manor Keep in return for keeping one royal falcon in permanent residence for the King. 'Not a bad bargain' said Mrs Saunders.

The house was used as a hunting box in 1922 and 1923 by The Prince of Wales, later King Edward VIII. Hunting was the favourite sport of his youth and, not surprisingly, he claimed one innovation in the matter of dress. He devised a knitted sleeveless sweater to take the place of the thick buttoned waistcoat which he found uncomfortable out hunting. He had his sweaters made in yellow to wear with a pink coat and grey to wear with a black one, but he does not relate what colour he wore with the Blue and Buff.[1]

[1] A Family Album by The Duke of Windsor. Cassell & Co. 1960 © Beaverbrook Newspapers Ltd.

RUNNING NEAR WESTONBIRT - Mr Toby Sturgis, then Saturday Field Master, is on the left of the picture.

TO THE NEXT DRAW - Bunched closely together the field moves to the next draw. Note the different types of headgear worn out hunting today.

THE PERFECT HAT - In 'A Leicestershire Sketch Book' (1935)
Lionel Edwards used this title 'cribbed from Ogilvie's poem' for a
sketch of the Belvoir, then under Captain Marshall Roberts'
Mastership.

It was the only occasion that a hunt was produced to order for the
artist's benefit and the Whipper-in was depicted holding up his hat as
the fox went away.

In this case, I saw the fox myself and the Perfect Hat is Charles
Wheeler's.

'THERE HE GOES' - The hunted fox seen from Mr Tim Smith's Land Rover.

TOP HATS TO THE FORE - Although the safety factor in favour of 'crash hats' cannot be denied, a silk top hat properly worn, takes some beating. It may not be safe, or even practical ... but it looks great. And a gentleman can take it off, not only to greet the Master, but to a lady, too. It will be sad if these old world courtesies fade, but I suppose now that the 'British Standard' helmet has arrived for both cricket and riding, it is inevitable. Happily, we have two traditionalists here and what a pleasure it is to see them.

THE BEAUFORT WALL - Seemingly suspended motionless in mid-air a lone rider tackles a Beaufort wall. The walls of Cotswold stone, neatly laid 'dry' are one of the key features of the country. This one is near Sopworth.

FIRST CLASS TRAVEL - Charles Wheeler riding a typical generous Irish bred hunter from the Badminton stable. This is his second horse on a day from Sherston. The Beaufort hunt staff are always well mounted and the horses look splendid.

THE REPAIR TEAM - The Beaufort Hunt Repair Team in action.
They are out every day and try to repair damage as it happens, even to
the extent of having the frustrating task of mending the same gap twice
in one day.

FAMILY AFFAIR - A Beaufort Hunting farmer, Joe Collingborn pictured with his family in Thursday country. Many farmers hunt on Thursdays, take great pride in their country, and have a lot of fun. Joe clearly believes in getting his family started young.

DRAWING KALE - Drawing the Monday Field Master's kale. Foxes love kale - always attributed to the fact that although it is very wet, it has a high bug and slug population. Tetbury Church is in the background.

GONE AWAY! - The Monday Field Master, Robin Ingall (second from right) leads the field away near Chavenage.

THE HUNTING FARMER - *Anthony Trollope wrote in* Hunting Sketches *as long ago as 1865:*

*   'Few hunting men calculate how much they owe to the hunting farmer, or recognise the fact that hunting farmers contribute more than any other class of sportsman towards the maintenance of the sport. It is hardly too much to say that hunting would be impossible if farmers did not hunt.'*

*   Trollope, in his autobiography, confessed he had written on many subjects 'but on no subject with such delight as that of hunting'.*

*   One farmer who delights in hunting and makes a great contribution is David Hibbard of Widleys Farm, Sherston. He was photographed at the moment he heard a holloa to signal a fox away. The grey's keenly pricked ears show that he has heard it, too.*

FARMERS - Three Beaufort farmers talk hunting at covertside on the Badminton Estate. Easily distinguished in their hunt caps and black coats, with black buttons engraved BH in white, they wear this dress with pride.

FARMER'S DAUGHTER - Sue Godwin, whose father farms near Luckington, has inherited a love of hunting from her grandfather, Bert Pateman, Kennel Huntsman to the Duke of Beaufort for thirty years. She received her Hunt button from the 10th Duke aged fifteen. She admits to having had a few bangs on the head, but she adores riding across country saying 'It's great if you get it right'. Her enthusiasm extends the year round, for she has made two visits to the Ellerslie Hunt in Australia where jumping wire was standard practice.

SIDE-SADDLE - Urged go try side-saddle by her husband, Mrs Pope confessed that she made little progress until she went for a fortnight to Lt. Colonel Jack Hance at Malvern, the first residential riding school in England. From then on she never looked back, receiving the 'Blue and Buff' from the Duchess before the end of her first season in 1939. Still hunting fifty-two years on, Mrs Pope acknowledged 'I owe everything to Jack Hance - he got me going'.

There was a time when girls no longer rode astride after the age of twelve and side-saddle elegance was the feature of the Beaufort field. Today, Mrs Pope and Mrs Pitman hunt regularly and continue to delight the eye.

To hunt side-saddle, you need a good horse that moves well - and a saddle that fits, for the risk of sore backs offers a special challenge to the saddler.

A TRADITION PRESERVED - Mrs Pope's granddaughter, Henrietta, continues the family tradition by riding side-saddle with the Duke of Beaufort's. She is seen here with her father, James Pope and her grandmother, at a meet at Chavenage. Both Henrietta and her sister Annabel, are members of the flourishing Side-Saddle Association and enter for competitions.

AN INSPIRATION - Having admired Mrs Cynthia Pitman and indeed tried to capture something of her elegance and style in a photograph, I asked Brian Higham about her.

'It's an inspiration to see Mrs Pitman,' he enthused 'she's always beautifully turned out, she rides straight, on good horses, and goes really well - and yet she's always got time to have a kind word. It would be good if the young ones of today took a leaf out of her book.'

ASTRIDE - In spite of its elegance, many women were happy to settle for the ease of riding astride when side-saddle was no longer de rigeur. And Auriol Culverwell looks good in the Blue and Buff style of today.

Auriol, although brought up in the Beaufort Saturday country, now lives and works in London but says she couldn't do it without getting away at week-ends. She likes to be involved with the day's hunting especially when she's asked to do point duty. She admits the Beaufort field is so big it is easy to lose track of what is going on, but she knows her home country very well and it's a big advantage.

The Duke Inn, Hillmarton.

LARGE THRONG, GENEROUS HOST - Captain Farquhar turns to thank his host, Richard Meade, for his hospitality after this Wednesday meet at Church Farm, West Littleton.

WEDNESDAY COUNTRY - Captain Farquhar, horn in hand,
watches hounds hunting near West Kington.

THE FIRST FLIGHT - Leading members of the Beaufort field. In the centre of the group is the Hunt Chairman, Antony Brassey.

OVER THE STUBBBLE - A fine November morning for the Wednesday field who are enjoying a quick start to the day.

THE EMPTY SADDLE - A fall brings the added complication of a fresh, fit, riderless horse. But Mrs Antony Brassey gallantly comes to the rescue.

GATE PLEASE! - The field tightly packed into a gateway. It looks a proper jam, but hounds are not running and horses and riders appear calmly unconcerned.

GOING HOME - The title reminded me of Will. H. Ogilvie's poem:
But the longest lane must turn
And the longest day must end;
And the stable lanterns burn
And the well-known roofs befriend.
And who that would not ride,
And who that would not roam,
For a lodge gate open wide
On the long hack home?

RIDING THE HEADLAND - John White, the Thursday Field Master, leads the field around the headland. Although there is much more plough in the Beaufort country these days, the Hunt is adapting to change, and opening up new country.

M4 - *The M4 motorway, slicing through Beaufort country, must have brought the late Duke and Major Gundry near to despair. But this photograph shows more than any other, the Hunt's ability to overcome difficulties. Noel Coward's simple advice to anyone in a show that failed was 'Forge ahead and rise above it'. And The Duke of Beaufort's Hunt, in a different kind of entertainment business, did just that. A hound proof fence was put up and a team of dedicated supporters volunteered to inspect and maintain it.*

The picture shows how close the hunt can come to the motorway. Hounds have run a fox to ground. Captain Farquhar has dismounted. The figure on the brown horse in the foreground is Toby Sturgis

BEAUFORT COUNTRY

THE HUNTING CORRESPONDENT - Foxford (Michael Clayton, Editor of **Horse and Hound**) enjoying a day with the Beaufort. He recalls that he had a good hunt in the afternoon, and having visited the Duke of Beaufort's intermittently over the past thirty years, said 'It is marvellous that the present Mastership manages to maintain such high standards in these difficult times.'

OVER THE GRASS - Leading members of the Beaufort field enjoying the ride over the grass near Sherston. Mrs Ian Farquhar is on the left nearest the camera.

BLOWING OUT OF COVER - There are different notes on the horn - some calls for hounds, some for the field. There is a book and record **Hunting by Ear,** *by Michael Berry and D.W.E. Brock (1949), featuring the Pytchley Huntsman, Stanley Barker explaining the music of the huntsman's horn and voice. This, I note, was still available from that doyen of all horse booksellers, Mr J.A. Allen, in his catalogue marked 'A Miscellany of Out of Print Books'. But whether it's blowing 'out of cover', or Mozart's Concerto, horn players sound different, so you have to know an individual huntsman's calls.*

CROSS-COUNTRY - Mrs Toby Sturgis, a former event rider and one of the best in the Beaufort field - crossing the wall country near Didmarton.

For some, second horses provide a most welcome break, while for others it is a busy time - meeting the horses, and making the change that brings a fresh impetus to the day.

THE HUNT CHAIRMAN - Antony Brassey, who is also a Wednesday Field Master, leads the field at the start of a day from Horton. Mr Brassey succeeded his father, the late Col. Sir Hugh Brassey, as Hunt Chairman in 1984 but his family connection with The Beaufort goes back seventy years, when his grandfather was on the Committee. His mother is the daughter of Captain Maurice Kingscote. It was Captain Kingscote who, with Mr Herbert Nell, whipped-in to the late Duke of Beaufort when he began hunting a small bitch pack two days a week in 1920.

Antony Brassey's contribution has been especially important. In 1984 he paved the way for the changes in organisation and style needed to make Captain Farquhar's Mastership the success that it has undoubtedly been. Three years later he had the task of getting the secretarial side newly established on the retirement of Major Dallas.

These inevitable changes have put the Hunt on a new footing although the establishment remains the same. Antony Brassey is enthusiastic about Ian Farquhar's drive to get more young people hunting, and that they should enjoy closer involvement with the hounds. He, the Farquhars, and the other Field Masters, have children between the ages of six and sixteen and they are all hunting.

And he adds 'we have returned to hunting regularly in the Sodbury Vale, the real old-fashioned country loved by Master as a young man. And the farmers in the Vale, many with small in-hand farms, have been very good to us, allowing us to ride over some of the Beaufort's most unspoilt natural country. But the lynch pin is Ian with his style of hounds and hunting . . . while the highest praise comes from some of the older hunting farmers who say it is as good now as it has been for twenty-five years'.

Seeing the Beaufort today, one gets this strong feeling of enthusiasm and fun. There's less emphasis on the social side. Perhaps that's a good thing - when I asked my aunt what it was like to hunt with the Beaufort in the 1920s she replied, 'Oh, they were very snooty'.

'NOT FOR THE FAINT-HEARTED' - The country near Horton is completely natural, with big fences. It's stiffer to cross but you have options - a wall, a hunt jump, or you can settle for the road which, if faced with a hedge and ditch this size, many might think the wisest choice.

120

'WHERE IS EVERYBODY?' - *The plaintiff cry of the hound left behind . . . but she needn't worry for in her heart she knows that Giles Wheeler will be along to collect her.*

THE OPPORTUNISTS - Thirsty hounds snatch a drink before going on to the next draw. It's thirsty work . . . hounds may travel up to a hundred miles in a day, and be out for six hours.

THE MORNING AFTER - Snoozing after an arduous seven hour day in the field, these tired hounds snuggle together in their warm straw. They barely stir at an unusual wake up call - a camera's electronic flash.

PUPPY WALKER - Farthing, the bitch puppy at walk with Julie Hoskins, will not be left out as her mistress leaves home on a a hunting morning.

Puppies are sent out to walk when six to eight weeks old, 'You're handed this fluffy little thing which grows up fast into a bundle of trouble, especially where the garden is concerned. Every plant is dug up' said Julie.

Puppy walking is a labour of love. They demand a lot of attention, exercise, feeding - and they chase everything. Wellington boots, car seat covers, clothes, turn up in most unlikely places. Washing lines are devastated. In one instance, a puppy was returned to the Kennels because of its desire to chew through the mains electric cable.

Walking a puppy brings the benefit of early human contact, saves the Hunt money, and gives the walker a great thrill if a prize is won at the Puppy Show.

THE FRIENDLY HOUNDS - Although the puppies return to the strict routine of the Kennels, they retain a friendly, some would say overfriendly, greeting for adults and children alike.

A PROFESSIONAL'S FAREWELL - On Brian Gupwell's last day, scarlet coats rare in Beaufort country, mix with the tawny yellow of the Berkeley, as his fellow professionals turn out in his honour, and to say goodbye. Brian is on the left as Captain Farquhar brings hounds off the Acton Turville road. He carries the good wishes of all after twenty-two years with the Beaufort.

THE UNSEEN GETAWAY - This fox makes good use of what military men call 'dead ground'. He might have escaped unseen but this is where car followers come in useful, and it's what they love. A delighted holloa, and hounds soon hit the line.

FLYING FOX - This fox was at full speed - and full stretch - as it shot past. But the photograph shows something of the energy and effort required when hounds are too close for comfort.

127

'One Fox on foot more diversion will bring
Than twice twenty thousand Cock pheasants on wing'
R.E. Egerton Warburton

' . . . but the hound must possess nose, stoutness, speed, courage and a number of valuable qualities which may be briefly summed up under the head of intelligence'.

The late Duke of Beaufort quoting his grandfather in his book Foxhunting (1980).

'There's a whistle away, and a cap in the air
But never a fuss or a scene:
The Blue and Buff squadron intend to be there -
Those men who can ride and those ladies so fair,
Who follow the huntsman in green.'

W. Philpotts Williams' poem appeared in Baily's Magazine in
December 1896. But this is December 1991 and a fox has gone away
from Sopworth.

ENCOURAGING THE CHILDREN - The Hunt encourages children as much as possible although they must not be unaccompanied until they are thoroughly competent. But they are well looked after and one mother goes as far as offering a meals on wheels service.

The Hunt has a large Pony Club with two hundred and seventy members, sixty-five of whom are boys. It has six areas, with area managers responsible, and organises many events including an instructional week in July.

THE YOUNG ENTRY - Known as 'the White Mice' the Misses Sturgis and Farquhar out hunting in Badminton Park.

EVENTERS - Ginny Leng and Lizzie Purbrick out hunting. Ginny is riding Priceless on which she won the Badminton, European and World Championships.

JANE HOLDERNESS-RODDAM - *At a meet of the Duke of Beaufort's at West Littleton. A member of the Gold Medal winning team in the Mexico Olympics 1968, and twice winner at Badminton, Jane believes hunting is invaluable for event horses: 'They can learn so much . . . turning, stopping, starting, staying balanced . . . and they learn faster, too. Hunting's a wonderful preparation'.*

RICHARD MEADE, OBE - *Holder of the Olympic individual and two team gold medals, Richard Meade had the honour of carrying the flag and leading the British team into the arena at the Closing Ceremony of the Olympic Games. Now retired from competitive riding he much enjoys hunting regularly with the Beaufort. He is seen here on a Wednesday at the National Westminster Bank's meet at Chipping Sodbury.*

Like the other eventers, he confirms that hunting has an important part in preparing horses and riders for the big occasion. He is convinced that his experience riding to hounds as a child gave him the confidence and security to win later on.

FANATICAL FOXHUNTER - *Richard's son, James, aged ten, frustrated as fog ruins a November Saturday. Described as 'fanatical about hunting', this is hardly surprising for his mother is a member of the Farquhar family.*

GONE TO GROUND - Hounds have run a fox to ground from Hyam Wood. The Hunt Staff have dismounted to investigate. The gentleman in the top hat holding the horse is Peter Sidebottom, the Saturday Field Master.

WASHING OFF - The Badminton lake, soon to be the scene of Cross-Country Day crowds and drama, provides an easy solution to the problem of removing Beaufort country mud. And it's much simpler than having to get the hosepipe out at home.

*SILHOUETTES AT SUNDOWN - A photograph taken on a Saturday
near Alderton.*

THE POINT-TO-POINT - The Members Race over Natural Country:
The competitors are seen at the first fence.

THE WINNER - Mr. David Akerman is seen receiving the Dick Horton Perpetual Challenge Cup from His Grace The Duke of Beaufort. David Akerman's triumph was all the more remarkable since he lost a leg in an accident.

140

HUNT CLUB SERVICE - Rosemary White received a gold bracelet from Her Grace The Duchess of Beaufort in recognition of her long service as Hon. Secretary of the Beaufort Hunt Club which has twelve hundred members 'we are able to support the Hunt well and have a lot of fun doing it' said Rosemary.

THE CROWD - Green Wellies!

HILL HUNTING - *After the Point-to-Point, on the first Saturday in March, hunting continues in the hill country, followers forsaking their blue and buff in favour of the tweed coat of 'ratcatcher', as worn by the well-turned out mounted Point-to-Point stewards pictured above.*

The photograph opposite was taken after a meet at the Blathwayt Arms, Lansdown, near Bath.

THE HUNTER'S MOON
'Night grows day for him,
Long wet lanes with her smile are strewn
Cares make way for him -
Him that for love hath the Hunter's Moon'
Will H. Ogilvie

'GOODNIGHT!'